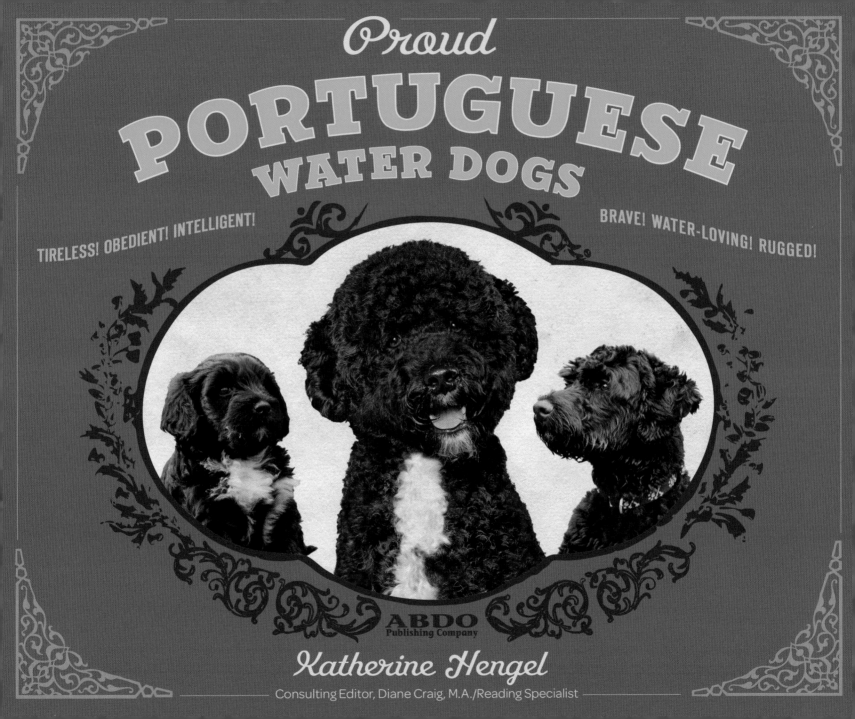

Proud
PORTUGUESE
WATER DOGS

TIRELESS! OBEDIENT! INTELLIGENT!

BRAVE! WATER-LOVING! RUGGED!

ABDO
Publishing Company

Katherine Hengel

Consulting Editor, Diane Craig, M.A./Reading Specialist

Published by ABDO Publishing Company
8000 West 78th Street, Edina, Minnesota 55439.

Printed in the United States of America,
North Mankato, Minnesota
052010
092010

♲ PRINTED ON RECYCLED PAPER

Editor: Liz Salzmann
Content Developer: Nancy Tuminelly
Cover and Interior Design and Production:
   Anders Hanson, Mighty Media
Illustrations: Bob Doucet
Photo Credits: Dreamstime (Chantal Ringuette, Manon
Ringuette), Fotalia (cynoclub, Zottelhund), ShutterStock

Library of Congress Cataloging-in-Publication Data
Hengel, Katherine.
 Proud portuguese water dogs / by Katherine Hengel ;
illustrated by Bob Doucet.
   p. cm. -- (Dog daze)
 ISBN 978-1-61613-380-1
 1. Portuguese water dog--Juvenile literature. I. Doucet,
Bob, ill. II. Title.
 SF429.P87H455 2011
 636.73--dc22
                    2010001835

CONTENTS

The
PORTUGUESE WATER DOG

Portuguese water dogs are excellent swimmers. They were **bred** to help Portuguese fisherman on their boats. These spirited dogs would **retrieve** torn nets and herd fish. They would even carry messages back to shore! Today, Portuguese water dogs make great pets. They are beautiful, hardworking, and strong.

FACIAL FEATURES

Head

Portuguese water dogs have large, wide heads.

Teeth and Mouth

They have large **canine teeth** and strong jaws.

Eyes

Portuguese water dogs have round, medium-sized eyes. They have very good eyesight.

Ears

Portuguese water dogs have thin, heart-shaped ears. Their ears hang close to their heads.

BODY BASICS

Size

Portuguese water dogs weigh 35 to 60 pounds (16 to 27 kg). They are 17 to 23 inches (43 to 58 cm) tall.

Build

Portuguese water dogs have broad, deep chests. They are very **muscular** and strong.

Tail

The tail is thick at the base and thinner toward the end. Their tails help them swim and dive.

Legs and Feet

Portuguese water dogs have powerful, muscular legs. They have **webbed** feet to help them swim.

COAT & COLOR

Portuguese Water Dog Fur

Portuguese water dogs have a lot of thick fur! Their fur is waterproof. Their coats are usually black, brown, or white. They can also be black and white or brown and white. Their coats can be curly or wavy.

Portuguese water dogs do not **shed** very much. This makes them less likely to cause **allergies**. People with dog allergies are often okay around Portuguese water dogs.

WHITE FUR

WHITE COAT

BROWN FUR

BLACK FUR

Portuguese water dogs come in many different colors and coats. The photos here show just a few examples.

BROWN COAT

BLACK COAT

BLACK AND WHITE COAT

HEALTH & CARE

Life Span

Most Portuguese water dogs live about 10 to 14 years.

Grooming

Portuguese water dogs need to be brushed at least once a week. Otherwise, their coats will become **matted** which can be painful. They should be given a bath once a month.

Portuguese water dogs need to have their hair cut about every two months.

VET'S CHECKLIST

- Have your Portuguese water dog spayed or neutered. This will prevent unwanted puppies.

- Visit a vet for regular checkups.

- Clean your Portuguese water dog's teeth and ears once a week.

- Make sure your Portuguese water dog gets plenty of exercise in wide-open spaces.

- Trim your Portuguese water dog's nails about every six weeks.

EXERCISE & TRAINING

Activity Level

Portuguese water dogs have a lot of energy! They love **retrieving** things from the water. If they don't get enough exercise, they can become unhappy.

Obedience

Portuguese water dogs enjoy pleasing their owners. They are great dogs for people who like to train their pets. Portuguese water dogs are very smart and learn quickly.

A Few Things You'll Need

A **leash** lets your dog know that you are the boss. With a leash, you can guide your dog where you want it to go. Most cities require that dogs be on leashes when they are outside.

A **collar** is a strap that goes around your dog's neck. You can attach a leash to the collar to take your dog on walks. You should also attach an **identification tag** with your home address. If your dog ever gets lost, people will know where it lives.

Toys keep your dog healthy and happy. Dogs like to chase and chew on them.

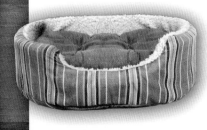

A **dog bed** will help your pet feel safe and comfortable at night.

ATTITUDE & INTELLIGENCE

Personality

Portuguese water dogs are fun to be around. They are dependable and brave. They love to play with other animals and children. It's rare to see a tired Portuguese water dog!

Intellect

Portuguese water dogs are very intelligent. They are easy to train and enjoy learning new things. They can learn to understand the words for many different objects. Portuguese water dogs try to be helpful.

All About Me

Hi! My name is Priscilla. I'm a Portuguese water dog. I just wanted to let you know a few things about me. I made some lists below of things I like and dislike.

Things I Like

- Going to the beach
- Swimming and diving
- Jogging with my owner
- Learning new tricks
- Playing fetch

Things I Dislike

- Staying inside all day
- Never being able to swim
- Being left alone
- Getting bored

LITTERS & PUPPIES

Litter Size

Female Portuguese water dogs usually give birth to four to eight puppies.

Diet

Newborn pups drink their mother's milk. They can begin to eat soft puppy food when they are about four weeks old.

Growth

Portuguese water dogs should stay with their mothers until they are eight weeks old. They reach their adult size when they are about two years old.

BUYING A PORTUGUESE WATER DOG

Choosing a Breeder

It's best to buy a puppy from a **breeder**, not a pet store. When you visit a dog breeder, ask to see the mother and father of the puppies. Make sure the parents are healthy, friendly, and well behaved.

Picking a Puppy

Choose a puppy that isn't too **aggressive** or too shy. If you crouch down, some of the puppies may want to play with you. One of them might be the right one for you!

Is It the Right Dog for You?

Buying a dog is a big decision. You'll want to make sure your new pet suits your lifestyle.

Get out a piece of paper. Draw a line down the middle.

Read the statements listed here. Each time you agree with a statement from the left column, make a mark on the left side of your paper. When you agree with a statement from the right column, make a mark on the right side of your paper.

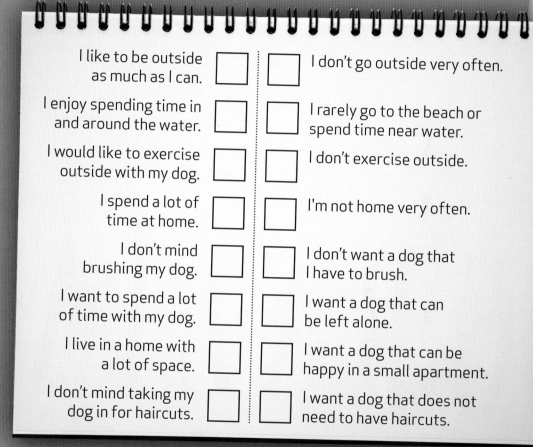

I like to be outside as much as I can.	I don't go outside very often.
I enjoy spending time in and around the water.	I rarely go to the beach or spend time near water.
I would like to exercise outside with my dog.	I don't exercise outside.
I spend a lot of time at home.	I'm not home very often.
I don't mind brushing my dog.	I don't want a dog that I have to brush.
I want to spend a lot of time with my dog.	I want a dog that can be left alone.
I live in a home with a lot of space.	I want a dog that can be happy in a small apartment.
I don't mind taking my dog in for haircuts.	I want a dog that does not need to have haircuts.

If you made more marks on the left side than on the right side, a Portuguese water dog may be the right dog for you! If you made more marks on the right side of your paper, you might want to consider another breed.

THE FISHERMAN'S BEST FRIEND

For hundreds of years, the Portuguese water dog was the fisherman's best friend. These hardworking dogs could even herd fish into nets! But by the 1930s, there were very few of them left. New ways of fishing had been invented. Fishermen didn't need their dogs as much as they once did.

That's when Vasco Bensaude decided to save the **breed**. He was a rich Portuguese businessman. He worked with local fisherman and veterinarians to breed Portuguese water dogs. Bensaude's dog, Leão, was the father of many Portuguese water dogs. Thanks to Bensaude and Leão, Portuguese water dogs are still with us today!

Tails of Lore
HOME RUN DOGS

Portuguese water dogs are excellent swimmers. But
did you know they are good at baseball too? In 2000, six
Portuguese water dogs formed the Baseball Aquatic Retrieval Korps
(B.A.R.K). Their job? **Retrieve** baseballs hit into the San Francisco Bay.

The San Francisco Giants are a Major League Baseball team. They play at AT&T Park, near the San Francisco Bay. Sometimes, a player hits a home run out of the park and into the water! The Portuguese water dogs in B.A.R.K. would fetch these "splash hits." Then the players who hit the balls would sign them. The balls were sold to raise money for local animal shelters.

FIND THE PORTUGUESE WATER DOG

A   B   C   D

THE PORTUGUESE WATER DOG QUIZ

1. Portuguese water dogs are poor swimmers. **True or false?**

2. Portuguese water dogs have very good eyesight. **True or false?**

3. Portuguese water dogs have **webbed** feet. **True or false?**

4. Portuguese water dogs **shed** a lot. **True or false?**

5. Portuguese water dogs do not need exercise. **True or false?**

6. Portuguese water dogs are very intelligent. **True or false?**

GLOSSARY

aggressive – likely to attack or confront.

allergy – sickness caused by touching, breathing, or eating certain things.

breed – 1. a group of animals with common ancestors. 2. to raise animals that have certain traits. A *breeder* is someone whose job is to breed certain animals.

canine tooth – one of four pointed front teeth of a mammal.

matted – full of thick tangles.

muscular – having well-developed muscles.

retrieve – to bring something back.

shed – to lose something, such as skin, leaves, or fur, through a natural process.

webbed – having skin connecting the fingers or toes.

About SUPER SANDCASTLE™

Bigger Books for Emerging Readers
Grades K–4

Created for library, classroom, and at-home use, Super SandCastle™ books support and engage young readers as they develop and build literacy skills and will increase their general knowledge about the world around them. Super SandCastle™ books are part of SandCastle,™ the leading preK–3 imprint for emerging and beginning readers. Super SandCastle™ features a larger trim size for more reading fun.

Let Us Know

Super SandCastle™ would like to hear your stories about reading this book. What was your favorite page? Was there something hard that you needed help with? Share the ups and downs of learning to read. We want to hear from you! Send us an e-mail.

sandcastle@abdopublishing.com

Contact us for a complete list of SandCastle,™ Super SandCastle,™ and other nonfiction and fiction titles from ABDO Publishing Company.

www.abdopublishing.com • 8000 West 78th Street Edina, MN 55439 • 800-800-1312 • 952-831-1632 fax